by Dominis

an anthology of unknown poet

2023.

Nikola Dominis

an anthology of unknown poet

Croatia

Mother I want to know

You Mary, you gave birth to God,
placed it in the poor manger,
probably your heart felt the pain
that like all other children, he
did not have his own crib,
you know, he loved the manger more,
so small and helpless,
but he was peaceful and secure,
because you and Joseph
have been watching over Him.

How you sung to him quietly,
how you hugged him,
when you would lift him on your knees,
and gently rocking him,
or when you would tell him those beautiful stories
about the old history, of Jewish,
and when you would hold him in your tender hands,
and kissed him, often you would shed a tear,
tear of happiness.

How wonderful are those early days for mothers,
how wonderful it is to have a baby,

those little hands that hug you
and big eyes that look at you,
let the universe pass, let the world end,
but mother does not see nothing but her child.

And there is something else
I would like to know,
Mother how is it up there among the stars,
how are you venerated by seraphims and cherubims
what is the Haven like when the angel's song arises,
and you shepherds tell me,
what kind of voice do angels have,
I would like to know that
and I would like to know how it is to be close to God,
how it is when you look at Him in the face,
how is it when His light illuminates you?

And a few more things I would like to know,
can I up there hear the song of the canary,
or happy swallows
as in the summer days in my homeland,
are up there as here
beautiful meadows and flowers,
are there any clear streams and high waterfalls,

I know I'm curious but I would like to know,

if I make it to you one day,
and you know I'll do my best to;
Will I ever see that joy of Bethlehem?
Will I be able to see little Christ?
And what was it like in the holy night?
You know, that's what I would like to know.

I know you hear me, Mother,
maybe your smile was elicited by
my child's desire,
but we were all childrens once,
we were all joys of our mothers,
although I'm not a kid anymore,
I would be sorry
to extinguish my childish dreams in me,
let it remain some of the joys of childhood,
let it remain some memory of smallness,
let it remain a bit of Christmas in me.

I will create

I will create a new world,
new rivers, new hills,
new flower in hand curled,
thousand horses the field fills.

I will create dreams by hand,
there will be no tears,
full of wonders my new land,
happiness without fears.

I will create works in my head,
in that wonderful land,
where no man's foot shall tread,
just my world my friend.

The world I will create from dreams
a world without any nightmare,
such a book I will create it seems,
you have to read it if you care.

In the beginning

You are bigger and older than the universe,
and a billion galaxies,
and those closest - "Andromeda",
and those far away hundreds of millions
light years.
You were there when they were born,
before a bit more than
thirteen billion years,
then in the mist of prehistory
you liquated stars and worlds,
shaped them, built them.
Yes, You, It was You,
when there was no time yet,
You told him to start,
You commanded him to set in motion,
You, It was You,
in the daybreak of history
You've created everything from nothing...
"When I consider thy heavens, the work of thy fingers,
the moon and the stars, which thou hast ordained; What
is man, that thou art mindful of him? And the son of man,
that thou visitest him?"

I would give everything

How I'd be happy to help
to you, brothers who suffer,
oh, how I would be happy if I were given the words
that fill with enthusiasm,
to be given the words which move the world,
how I'd wish for people to listen, to hear,
these politicians, rulers, people with power,
the mighty ones of the world to gain grace
to see, to feel,
to understand the pain of a mother
whose child is dying of hunger,
the pain of a father whose princess
longs for a drop of water.

Oh, wake me up tomorrow
and tell me they've understood,
wake me up and tell me the new day is coming,
day of light that doesn't know of sunset,
day ruled by Christ.
What we did to the smallest ones,
we dif to Him, and to ourselves!

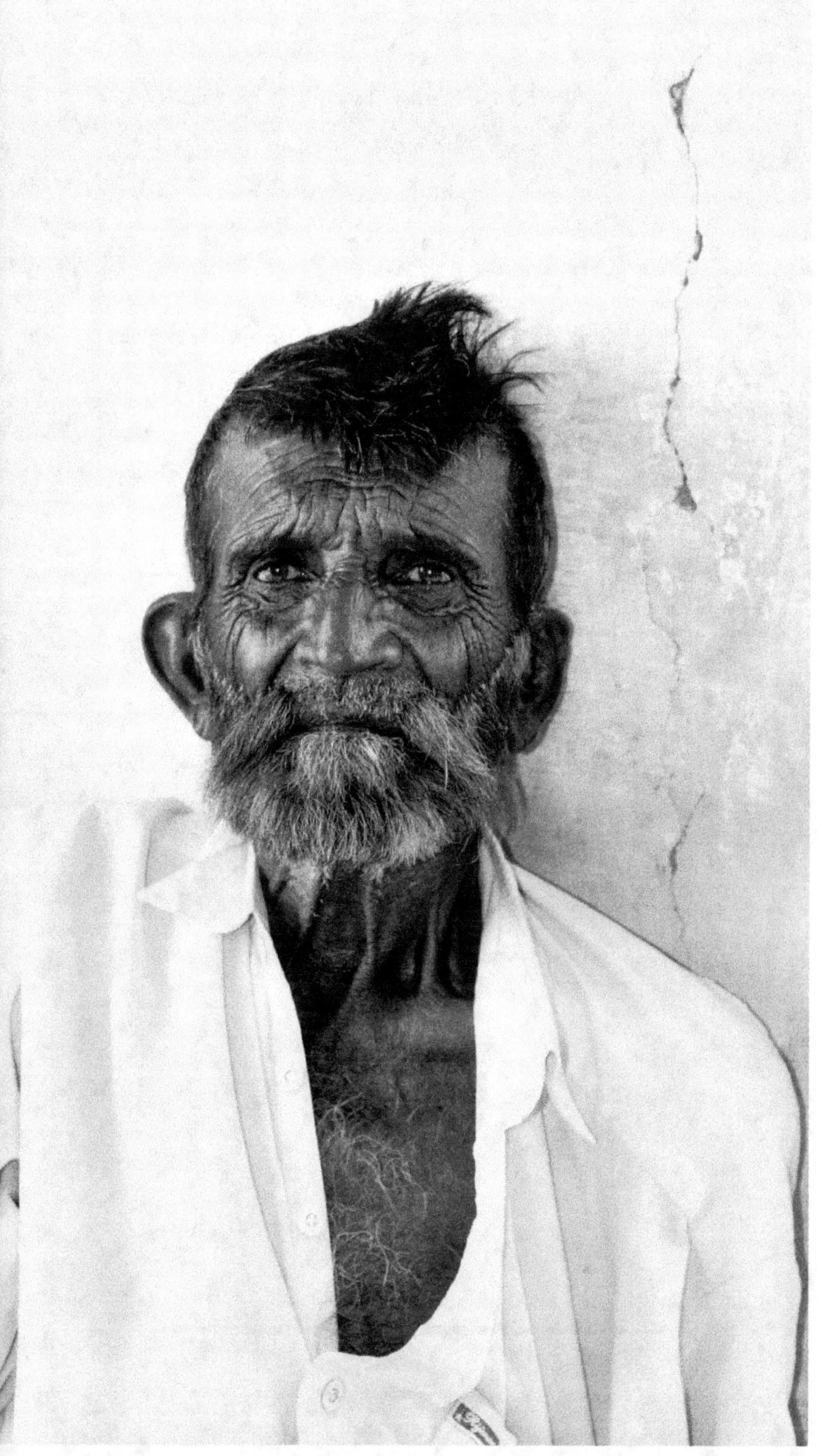

Indeed, I would...I would if I could,
give all the money of the world
for a single drop of mercy
to the little ones!

It's value is more than that of pearls and gold,
worth more than all the treasures
of this grand world,
and the whole universe is worthless compared to it!

Oh, wake me up tomorrow
and tell me that they understand!

Space Traveler

I lay on the lawn,
one warm August night,
I watch the night filled with stars,
it tells the story about the Creator,
a Traveler who travels through the universe,
who plays with stars,
about the One who created them.

I pass through the transparency of the universe,
I follow traces of Brother Moon,
I listen to the echo, which quietly repeats:
Praise...Praise the Lord.

The universe is not empty,
the universe is not cold,
this whole universe is in God,
and God is in it,
I listen to the voice in admiration,
the evening is quiet,
but starry sky
speaks a lot to me.

I travel aswell,
it's time to go,
infinity calls me there,
there at the end of the earthly,
at the end of matter,
beyond the body,
in a silent prayer,
where Heaven begins.

Saint Damien De Veuster

Oh, there's no such a hero from far away,
He dreamt to be like the flanders lion,
little Joseph wanted to kill dragon
or giant or something like that,
and he also wanted to become a pope.

But he realized very quickly
that heroes don't have to be big
he also realized that big people
don't have to be always large and strong
he realized
that mother who's giving her best to
raise her children is a hero,
and that father who's working hard
to feed all the hungry mouths is a hero,

And that you can become
a hero in a desert, and in a
solitary chamber.
He finished the schools,
he was named Damien,
and he went to the missions,

in the heavenly archipelago of Hawaii,
there was a place more like hell.
Molokai, island of refugees,
island of lepers.

It was a hell until he came there,
the hero of Flanders,
oh, how the wounds were stinking,
how hard it was
to look at the decomposing faces,
and the limbs with only stumps left on.
But that's the way to become a hero, isn't it?
And in the end he himself gave a sacrifice
as he himself said:
If God gives me, I will carry Your cross also,
I will be leper among lepers.

And at his funeral it was written on the cross:
Greater love hath no man than this,
that a man lay down his life for his friends.

That day, the world and the heaven,
They got a new hero,
and what a great, holy hero.

Ideal

He is far away,
many will say,
why to fervor,
when it's impossible,
nice,
but impossible.

I tell you men
everything is possible
to the one who believes,
the ideal is in you,
believe in it.

Ideal is the voice,
the voice in your heart,
ideal is the fervor,
fervor that wins,
ideal is the future,
achievable future.

The ideal is a viewpoint,
on which we have to climb,
ideal is a compass,

which directs us,
the ideal is the strength,
which has to bear us,
ideal is life
which has to be lived.

Life

You can become someone...
You can choose millions of wonderful things...
You can become...
Aviator...
Dreamer...
Woodcutter...
Poet...
Saint...

There is only one prerequisite...

Life...
That wonderful gift,
worth every wonder...

You

You will be created as a product of a fairy tale,
I will weave you of flowers and rhyme,
without father and mother you will wail,
the Child of dreams is your name for this time.

I will know you by the tapping of the rain,
and you will be like the mystic herself,
queen of the empire, sometimes and thane,
a bandit girl, but more often the elf.

You'll know how to play in the mud,
like a country girl, and so beautiful,
in the Great War you will be scud,
you will always be simple, immutable.

And you will never, never leave me,
no matter how angry fate has befallen us,
a picture of a holy woman you will be
to the end of the road without discuss.

Then I will give everyone a free hand,
there will be no chase not even after me,
misfortunes and torments will be manned
and someone else will give fairy tales humanity.

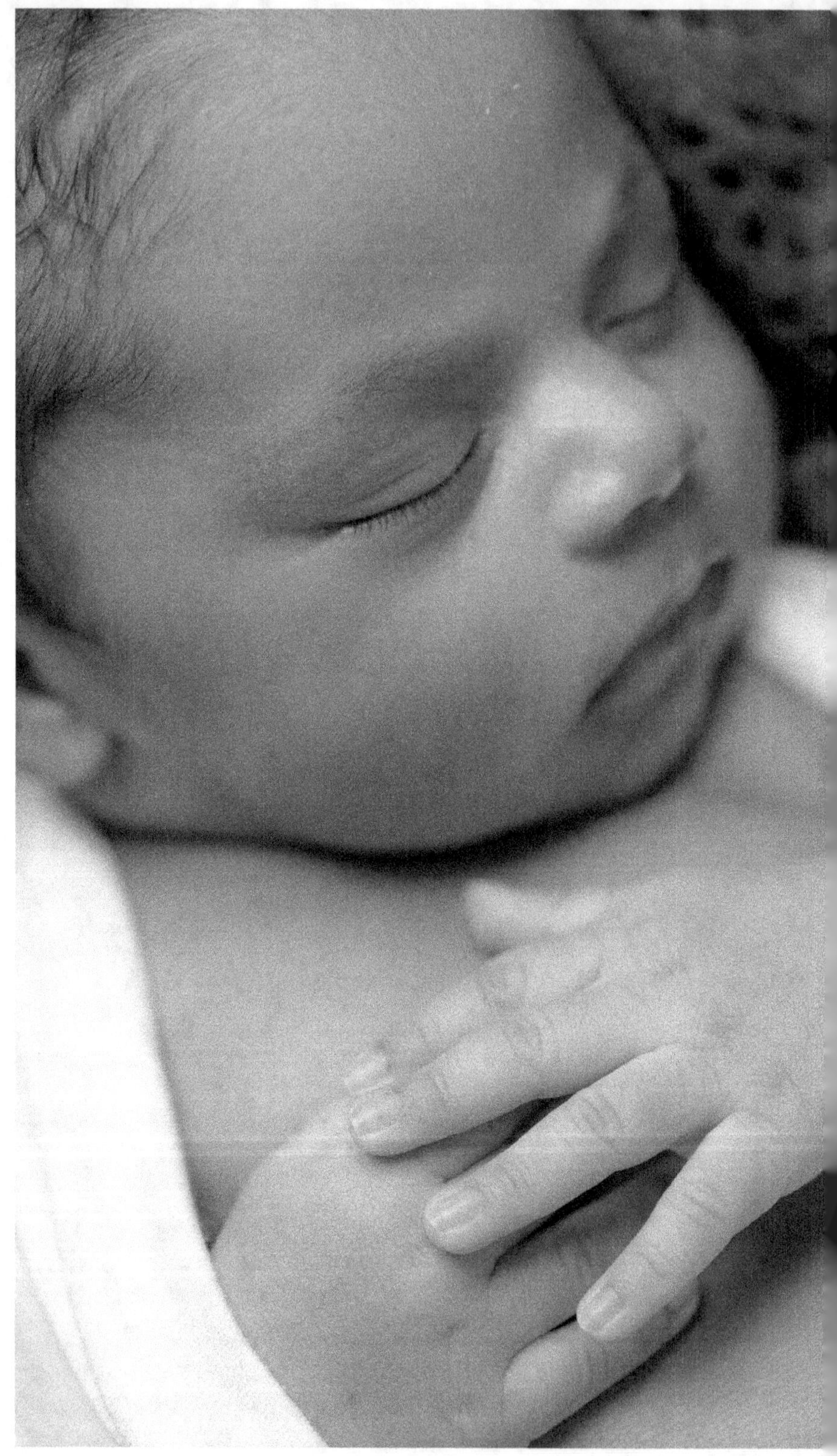

What I would do

Ah what I would do if I had not been born,
I would not know God who is love,
I would not be able to play,
not watch the stars!

Ah what I would do if I had not been born,
what if I didn't get a chance,
all that would remain would be
a longing for life,
something like a dream in the late morning.

Ah happy me to be born,
now I can bend planes of newsprint,
can shoot with laughter
and rejoice in a thousand ways,
really, happy me,
because now I can make people happy,
and now I can conquer Paradise.

An ode to peace

Again he wandered the trenches last night,
where peace has been quietly hidden since the war,
and he begged the time not to bite,
the mother prayed to see her son alive and swore.

He wandered again last night where he was hiding
the most beautiful stars full of brilliance,
I see a sweet child swaying
on the sunny swings of our county as it was once.

In the quiet sky where the stars are counted,
I saw many bodies was shaking,
I saw brave fighters afraid to accounted,
at a bloody feast in a mad dance chancing.

Oh, how sweet everything is with peace,
who can now count all the victims,
ah the misfortunes that befall us caprice,
I say, the dead are not counted victor's.

Cursed be everyone who calls for wars,
and who plays the game of life and death,
now heroes lay dirty with mud, full of sores,
to whom happiness, to whom mega-death.

Stop the wars to be clear,
prevent the sea of tears from ever flowing,
let the president and every government hear,
Due to you the smell of death is blowing.

Mystique

Through the mist, a man passes,
does not see the way, does not see the path,
he moves forward because he is a tracer and a traveler,
he strives for the indescribable,
he listens to the silence,
and understands the breeze which speaks to him about
God,
and approaches the Bush that Burns, but does not
Burn Out,
and admires the nature and everything that God has
created,
and is astonished with man and his unfaithfulness
he is blessed even though he does not see, but still
believes,
even if sometimes he does see, he keeps searching for
more
he prays to the Holy One and strives for holiness
he speaks of something that words cannot describe
he feels and knows that has to be it
because he is a mystique of the modern age.

Puppets

Oh darling, what kind of puppets are we in the theater of
dreams,
and who pulls our strings,
the hidden hands of some gray eminences,
unfortunate fates of sad plays,
and how happy we were,
that summer, in the sunny hours of our youth,
don't forget me
and if we never see each other again
and if our paths never intertwine again,
it doesn't matter, something will remain of that feeling,
and you will be replaced by her, better,
and I will be replaced by someone, maybe make you
happy,
and what has been, let it be
we are innocent puppets in a bloodthirsty world,
and difficult destinies are our reality,
and all these years an illusion.

Stone pillar

A stone pillar stood
in the courtyard of Pilate's court.

He didn't want that,
but its beautiful structure
it was tarnished by purpose,
it is not a stone created to torment,
he was created to delight with his beauty
that under the hand of an artist
creates the most beautiful sculptures,
he was created to build houses
and high proud pillars
which shines for thousands of years,
not to tie the hands of the wounded,
not to absorb the blood of the convicts.

The pillar knew many sufferings,
but this one was too hard,
the suffering of the innocent has always affected him,
but the suffering of this man, and of God,
he couldn't figure out why they were doing this to him,
he heard only words of praise about Him,

while the soldiers spoke softly,
he only heard touching and wonderful stories about Him,
everyone was saying it couldn't be
than an supernatural being.

And you chains, come on, let him fly away,
to fly away into the distant sky, into freedom like a bird.
Oh, if only I were like you made of iron,
to forge the sharpest sword out of me,
how could I just defend him, you know,
send, send Archangel Michael,
and the army to defend him,
but He will not.
he has to do this himself,
this is the most difficult case,
He has to pay for your place.

These times

You dream of those times,
the same foreboding flickers,
that our days will again become those time,
a new bell has been ringing in the church for a long time
will chime,
and we mi, we're just a little more serious fools,
who dream the same dreams
but never again as in schools,
the same dreams full of the most sublime beings,
which take us away from
earthly bloodshed and these things,
who dream of a land without wars,
a land without ruined cities and open sores,
a land wrapped in dreams,
like a baby, innocent, asleep in a crib, it seems,
and we walk the street of freedom,
harsh weather, some falls without food and water, and I
need 'em,
we walk and think we're on top,
and we forget the most important things, the meaning
of our lives we will drop,
and we dream everything, we dream and walk on,

while reality drags us into

bloodthirsty jaws where it's all gone,

and the world is looking

at everything to get revenge on us,

and we walk..., we walk innocent, naive and holy without

undue fuss.

In winter nights

Zagreb's snow has brought down the last leaf,
she might have been drunk that night,
were days around Christmas,
she wanted only one thing
that someone listens to her in the winter nights,
to have someone to snuggle up to,
tears and dreams were alive,
no one knew her secret,
she loved but was never loved
she dreamed but was never dreamed,
she worked at a neighborhood bakery,
we would see each other sometimes
but since that day she has disappeared,
the sun in Zagreb was shining weaker,
the days began to swell,
and she was not there,
who knows maybe she left with butterflies,
maybe she moved to the sea
and there, with those beautiful eyes, he looks at the open
sea,
maybe she's happy
I'm just afraid that it might not be...

There, there in the fairy tale

I didn't look for you in the contours of reality,
you were a being from another world,
the being of the vast forests of misty Avalon
or that other island - Atlantis,
you lived in the mists of my memory from a young age,
maybe you were hiding
in the sunny cities of Hyperborea,
or among the tall pillars of Shambhala,
you are a myth, you are a queen, a child of a fairy tale,
you know that time when the stars were still sleeping
and I seem to know him with you,
where wind and rain become friends
there I will look for you, in the winter of our islands,
in the spring of our lost souls,
you will appear suddenly and out of nowhere,
you will know our language,
and to speak to thousands of others,
and when they ask you: What is love?
Like the Prophet,
you will answer that difficult question.
Love is a butterfly that lands on your

hand to delight you,
but butterflies are short lived. Love is the midday sun,
but in no time it will be dark.
And if that love touches you,
you, just you, a strange being
who reads these strange verses,
let go, Love made the universe move
in time before time,
Love..., eternal Love knew that one day,
in some late age of this small civilization
from a tiny planet in some remote part of the universe,
to connect many souls into one feeling,
and among them will be you and me,
as witnesses to an unfortunate love,
as witnesses of sad love
of the one God and his people.
And who can contradict me?
Who can say I'm talking nonsense?
One God – the best one – Jesus,
one world and one Love
but the dream has been given to us
and who knows in which world we drifted off to sleep,
and in which did we wake up?

Don't cry

Don't cry, when you hear I'm no longer near,
it's just your little golden one asleep here.

Don't cry, everyone must pass through this night,
these are just the last starry lights.

Don't cry, these stubborn poets can't truly die,
that's just the way they fly.

Don't cry, just let me spread my wings high,
I should land in a better sky.

Don't cry, even when the gloomy autumn will come,
it too shall pass, like every one.

Don't cry, light a single candle for me to view,
because I'll no longer light it with you.

Snowflake

Rise your eyes, just look, don't stare at the ground,
Lift your head, soar on wings of the finest birds' flight,
I count your tears like a tree's rings tightly wound,
Like the firs snow, you whisper, "it's just a snowflake so
light."

They flutter down, year after year, to the hollow below,
Full of old memories and dreams left unmet,
Yet there's a nostalgia, a beautiful ache they bestow,
Christmas is nearing, and a New Year will set.

Once more, snow will blanket us, trembling anew,
Once more with old dreams, the same fate will unfold,
How you should've fled, at least once, broken through,
From reasons so rational, to a flight brave and bold.

And when your back bends and your hair turns gray,
When you'd hardly recognize the lines on my face,
If childhood games returned, barefoot in snow you'd play,
A snowflake will glide from the sky, down your cheek wit
grace.

Her pain

She was beautiful.
Brown hair cascading over her face.
The only things noticeable
behind the hair were her eyes...
Those large, green eyes.
Eyes full of some mystical pain.
She tried to be normal in a crazy world.
She tried not to cause pain to anyone,
yet she carried the thick bitterness of fate...
A fate that was not kind to her.
Her mother left her while she was still a baby.
Her father remained but not for long;
drinking and vices cost him his life. And she...
She just wanted to be loved.
But Love, as if it had never heard of
the little beggar girl, was the only hope she had.
Hope – it never left her.
Not even when she lay sick and alone.
Not even when they left her because she didn't fit in.
Not even when her only shoes broke
and the rain was falling even more her soul...
Her soul... her soul was like the most precious gold.

Not gilded with a ton of expensive makeup,
but full, purified, and shining gold.
Of gold...

Candle

Last night,

at your grave,

without tears and flowers,

one already spent candle

lit up in late hours.

It's a sad sight,

casting melancholy shadows,

last night, on your grave,

one candle to its end it goes.

And I wouldn't swear

it wasn't stolen,

perhaps placed there

by a human shadow with soul in,

or maybe someone tragic,

a wanderer from the margins.

When I think about it,

I feel a sense of longing.

Do they wander here,

and as the last flame will be andel,

it sadly extinguishes,

the flame of a spent candle.

And it's as if with it,

from memory, it vanished,
when the last flame of candle
ceased to be banished.
Last night,
at your grave,
without tears and flowers,
one already spent candle
lit up in late hours.

Dreams of a Poet

I'll dream new dreams in
a land far away,
new poems will remain,
about a beautiful girl, I say.

My words will flicker
between fingers on an old guitar,
and she will wait for me there,
in some wondrous bookstore afar.

There, my words will mark,
prominently displayed,
like eyes that flash in the dark,
a destiny beautifully portrayed.

I'll rest silent in grave by then,
while she dreams of me,
each verse I've penned,
awakening her memorie.

Everything will be spoken,
my poetry appreciated,
to you, unknown beloved woman,
this poem is dedicated.

Under the Silver Moonlight

Under the silver moonlight,
the secret of the world we saw it,
but who would have known back then
that I would become a poet.

And that all the days would fit,
into those strange letters you see,
that by some miracle, a world
of dreams would come to be.

Who would have guessed,
that such a happy tale would unfold,
under the silver moonlight,
where that girl now shines like gold.

That girl will be entirely,
inscribed with my ink,
with sweet words in a peculiar script,
through of poems she will blink.

I've prepared words for her,
that will be read for centuries,
cold winters will turn warm,
and she'll delight in new springs.

All of this is still just a dream,
and these words sketches are mere,
what will create, I don't yet know,
this wanderer and this dreamer.

But it will be something valuable,
born in her honor I vower,
under the silver moonlight,
poetry holds all the power.

Come

Come, and we will conquer the Earth
and all its continents.
The world will revolve for us,
and it will know that we are somewhere far away...
Somewhere far away in open space
where we walk among the stars.
Come, speak, wink at me
like a real lady,
extinguish all the darkness in me with your light.
Don't look back, the world goes on,
but one day, in the end,
a memory will remain in the earth's crust
because we passed through there.
Let your foot take just the first step into the world,
agree, is it that hard,
and I will do everything else,
I will carry you through the ages.
And if anyone asks you about me,
toss it like a bone to a dog:
"What can I say? A poet."
I am ready to create for you
verses without equal,

words woven of love and dreams.
I am ready to put you on a pedestal
and, in the manner of the greatest poets,
sing of your beauty. So come,
come so I can love you.

The quest for love

We searched for each other on the paths of dry,

crumbling deserts.

There, in the terrifying jungles of metropolises.

As if the entire universe was on those narrow roads.

My nights were anxious and dark.

We searched for each other

on the outskirts because we were not among

those who live in high towers.

We were not there at all, neither alive nor dead.

And we found each other just a step from our homeland.

We found each other in the heart of a fire that still burns.

On the watery cradle with the rocking of waves.

And happiness gave birth to a new heart

a heart full – not of love – that so misunderstood word.

Happiness gave birth to something more than love –

eternity.

And we knew that it was born for us

seekers of new and still unknown feelings.

For you, the girl with the most beautiful eyes,

for me, a tragic figure in that great story.

For us, to whom everything was a thought...

A thought that scattered across the world,

and yet it never left us.

I will draw

Then I will write you your world with words
Because I cannot draw
But be warned –
Every sketch,
Every brushstroke,
Every final touch
Will feel like icy water on your skin.
And you know,
All will pivot towards the ground,
That mother of our bones.
In her womb,
For hundreds of years you will be.
We will laugh quietly
So no one hears us,
Perhaps hold hands.
If you go before me,
Let them turn your head
Toward the side
Where I will one day lie.
If I go before you,
Turn mine
Thus I can see in the dark those eyes, those hands.

I will draw, you'll see,
What a beautiful picture of rhymes
That the memory of you will last for eons.
What I leave behind will be based only on my words.
All my silver and gold.
But you will be remembered –
Happy and smiling,
You will be remembered,
For you are the depth of that golden gleam
The only image off some happy world,
A life we will never truly leave.
We will only change the ground beneath our feet
And the Light that will forever shine before us.

A sad sad song was coming once

This song was written once,
Completely, completely sad,
This song was written once,
And happiness remains indebted.

She came into being as a child
All human sorrows,
He smiled for no reason
Sad for many tomorrows.

Lots of tears, lots of pain,
And many sleepless nights,
All troubles come with rain,
God forbid I have a right.

They say all sorrows pass,
And that D minor is the saddest,
They don't know they have no class,
There is no chord for the baddest.

Many sorrows do not pass my chum,
And many tears flow forever,
You can only grieve with them,
Kiss wounds that don't heal but never.

Thus sorrow arises itself,
A very sad verse is written,
After all, I stayed with myself
Quite gloomy and inside bitten.

A sailor's death

At sunset he falls
into gloomy fate,
and darkness calls
after the first straight.

Now he can hear
His clock winding down,
Without kin, without near,
He roams town to town.

But new songs arise
From deep in his soul,
To eternal skies
The ship takes its toll.

Far from his home
And childhood dreams,
A mighty crash's foam
Leads him to the streams.

Silent and mute
He sank into night,
On the edge of pursuit
He went out of sight.

The dark ocean's deep
Now hides his boat,
He soars o'er the steep
With wings afloat.

Dead girl

I hear the weeping all around,
Funeral bells – I pray,
Oh, God, let it be anyone,
Let it not be her today.

And everything's gone awry,
So bleak, quieter each day,
All we once shared together
Is never, never to stay.

They take you there now,
As your body fades and fades,
Soon I'll follow the same path,
My hair already grays.

Oh, what a beauty she was,
But is this her here today?
That she was once alive,
The funeral bells now say.

I could even die

I rarely think of us,
And when I do, I feel like you no longer remember me.
You were everything to me, but what was I to you... who
knows?
Perhaps only the trees in front of your building,
That in those days
Saw you through your window,
Lost in thought, with a tear in your eye,
Staring at the clouds.
They say you never spoke of me,
And I, well, I stayed silent, mostly,
But for different reasons,
It hurt too much.
You kept living, and I,
You laughed again, and I,
I could even die,
Unnoticed.

Sleep tonight

Sleep tonight
in a cradle of woven reeds,
in Bethlehem's humble stall.
Sleep in peace,
for days will come soon enough
when all will be forgotten,
when for all your love
they will crown you with thorns.
Sleep, little God,
sleep just one more night,
for they do not know,
they still do not know
that history rests in your hands.
Sleep in peace,
let neither rain nor storm
disturb your gentle dream;
they will bow to you in time.
Sleep in peace,
But in the end, remember us.
Sleep tonight,
and we will keep vigil thus.

Jesus

He, the Child, will be the undefeatable conqueror of the
world
in conditions unworthy of a King
the future is born
and the blood brotherhood of man and God.

He, the little child, brings the mystery of love
the child teaches people how to live in the light
but he must, he must go through suffering
the day has ended, and the darkness grows.

The hills have opened their abysses
the cunning old serpent laughs from the abyss
with an unspoken malicious mockery
the whole hell laughs and sneers.

Will the serpent condemn Him, destroy Him
replace the daylight with the darkness of night
turn the meaning of love into hatred
will they put Him, the righteous, on the cross?

How did He come to this desolate, icy land
lost in a foreign world of desolation
from afar, the cry is heard:
"Father, let Your will be done."

The beautiful world woven from goodness is destroyed
the very core of love is destroyed
and the old cunning serpent laughs
while the Mother weeps, painfully and desperately calling
her Son.

Two beautiful worlds, the spiritual and the material
united in perfect harmony
and blood, for the salvation of humanity
blood for the sacrifice of our sins.

Hypocritical condemnation, betrayal for a handful of
coins
three times denied, He, the light of the world
they condemn Him, they crucify Him
thinking they seek life, but they find death.

They considered true life as death
because they did not understand it,
their hearts were hard, and He gives them His life
as a propitiatory sacrifice for the final light.

The world fell silent, the birds ceased
they withdrew into their depths
they wondered if He, perhaps, truly was the King
the head falls, "Into Your hands, I commit my spirit."

The pain is unbearable for those who denied Him
the sincerity makes it irresistibly sad
but now they are on the threshold, at the door of light
of gentle peace, of wonderful and holy peace.

They weep, and He weeps with them
these tears wipe away the impurity of the soul
they rebirth, they bring peace
He loves His enemies.

And after three days, He lives
He rose before the sun
fresh, intoxicated with the peace of dawn
He returned among the living, into the light.

The chirping of birds was heard
the joy of the world returned
the sun shone cheerfully the earth refreshed,
fragrant with the awakening.

Nothing can destroy Love anymore,
refined by the nobility of suffering
now He walks in the light, clothed and joyful,
He fulfilled His promise.

They learned the value they carry within
now they know that love is the life of the soul
now they know Him as He is
for the light You have given us, thank You, Jesus.

Poets of the 21st Century

Born on the edge,
in the belly of the suburbs,
at train stations bound for far-off places,
they pen verses on benches,
on crumbling walls they write of love.
Their words don't travel far;
their sweet thoughts win no awards,
but one thing must be acknowledged:
they capture hearts,
they inspire.

Their themes are those
of the spring sun,
whispering from above,
whispering of a better world,
whispering of love.
And who could scold them?
Who would stop them?

When love spreads
from heart to heart,
from East to West,

from South to North,
their song pierces through,
on a wave of joy that swells,
on a wave of hope stronger than all hatred.
The world will come to know them—
it must happen.
But what is fame?

Their mission is different:
to be the drivers of a world without divisions,
the pioneers of a civilization of love.

My Dreams

My dreams, you know,
are unlike in this world's streams,
I am the wind, the sea, a poet of dreams...

But know this, stranger girl,
one day, we'll meet face to face –
don't be surprised, don't lose your grace.

You'll know,
for only a woman can see
how to turn a man a piece of a dream – so it will be.

You'll know how
to take all my grey and sorrowed skies
and build a new world, in colours that rise.

And you alone will have the power
to push me forward when I stall,
to lift me up when I might fall.

But know,
for you, the world will cease its pace,
with the joy and heart, I'll place.

Poets are like this, you see –
you'll be my muse, my art,
and the world will weep with joy at heart.

Your happiness,
my greatest vow to embrace,
your love, my deepest thesis to trace.

Perhaps we'll wander
like nomads on distant trails,
laughing and living where hope prevails.

Perhaps we'll march,
on barricades, shoulder to shoulder we'll stand,
raising revolts against powers so grand.

Or perhaps we'll just
sail the world far and wide,
and bring back a flower from Burma, Nepal, side by side.

Maybe, maybe –
a thousand dreams may align,
perhaps a garden by a house that's ours and fine.

And at last, know this –
this is my wondrous plan
only love, love, love – our dream's true span.

Little Way

To be a child, yet strong and bright,
to be holy and a beacon of light,
to always be there for others in need,
this is the little way to Heaven.

When you start a journey, and can't see the end,
perhaps you're right at Heaven's bend,
pause for a moment, help your brother out,
this is the little way to Heaven.

When you see you're not doing great deeds,
just a big dream and big needs,
they carry you on this path so fine,
this is the little way to Heaven.

To be humble and be small not tied to a thing,
freely follow in Christ's footsteps, and sing,
where peace and love forevermore
this is the little way to Heaven.

That Night the Stars Fell

The last rays of the sun hid behind the horizon.

He remained in the cold, silent desolation.

Until now, he felt the warmth of the sun, but now...

No one pays attention to him, except the sky.

That night, the stars fell because of him.

They slid down the face of the night sky,

like shiny tears on the face of God.

They slid down out of sorrow;

they knew how long that night was for him.

Indeed, the stars fell,

because they knew he was suffering:

the poor, the homeless, and the vagrant from the slum.

People say he is just a bum.

But do they know anything about misery?

How to understand the pain of the street from a warm

home?

How to recognize that secret in front of the TV?

How can the full understand the difficulty of the hungry,

or the proud the pain of the humiliated and wretched?

Oh, rise up, man; you see that life is waiting for you.

Bring him food, brighten his long hours,

and don't say, "What does it matter to me?"

But make the end of his story beautiful.
Yes, on other nights the stars will fall,
but no longer because of the sorrow of the poorest.
Let there be tears of joy because of your wonderful
virtues.

Content:

www.ingramcontent.com/pod-product-compliance
Lightning Source LLC
Chambersburg PA
CBHW050825250726

48653CB00006B/2430